Imagine
a Planet where every
Child loves to Read.

Scholastic Book Fairs

Printed in U.S.A. © 1998 Scholastic Book Fairs

A Gift For ~~the Library~~

Given By: *BOOK Fair '99* Scholastic Book Fairs®

CIP data for this title is available from the Library of Congress

ISBN 0-525-65262-0

Published in the United States by Dutton Children's Books, a member of Penguin Putnam Inc., 375 Hudson Street, New York 10014

Conceived and produced by Breslich & Foss, London

Project editor: Janet Ravenscroft
Designer: Brian Wall
Additional artwork: Anthony Duke
Photography: Liam Muir

Printed in Singapore

First edition 10 9 8 7 6 5 4 3 2 1

PICTURE CREDITS

Breslich & Foss are grateful to the following individuals and institutions for permission to reproduce illustrations:
Ancient Art and Architecture Collection: p.5 (left and right), p.6 (bottom). Bridgeman Art Library, London/Biblioteca Medicea-Laurenziana, Florence: p.13 (bottom, death of Montezuma); /Bibliotheque Nationale, Paris: p.2 (top, dragons), p.3 (bottom, Marco Polo), p.4 (left, mythical animals), p.4 (right, wolf-headed people); /Kunsthistorisches Museum, Vienna: p.9 (Sir Francis Drake); /Louvre, Paris: p.3 (top left, bearded head pendant); /Mitchell Library, State Library of New South Wales: p.25 (left, koala); /Private Collection: p.20 (bottom, Livingstone); /Raymond O'Shea Gallery, London: p.7 (top, map of Pacific, China and America); /Royal Geographical Society, London: p.16 (top, Simia ursina), p.20 (top, the 'Ma Robert'), p.21 (top, the Great Western Fall). Dover Publications Inc.: p.18 (top). E.T. Archive, London: p.13 (top), p.25 (right); /Bibliotheque Nationale, Paris: p.3 (top right), p.7 (bottom); /British Museum, London: p.11 (bottom right); /Liebig card: p.27 (left); /NASA: p.29 (both); /Naval Museum, Madrid: p.10 (center); /Richmond Borough Council: p.19 (left). Mary Evans Picture Library: p.2 (bottom), p.8 (top and bottom left), p.10 (bottom), p.11 (bottom left), p.14 (top right and bottom left), p.15 (right), p.16 (bottom), p.18 (center), p.19 (right), p.21 (bottom), p.22, p.23, p.24 (both), p.26, p.27 (top and bottom right), p.28 (both); /Explorer: p.10 (top). York Archaeological Trust Excavation and Research Ltd: p.5 (bottom).

Front jacket courtesy of York Archaeological Trust Excavation and Research Ltd; Detail: Bridgeman Art Library, London/Raymond O'Shea Gallery, London: Map of the Pacific, China and America. Endpapers: E.T. Archive, London/Bibliotheque Nationale, Paris.

THE
Explorer's
HANDBOOK

MARILYN TOLHURST

HOW TO BECOME AN INTREPID VOYAGER

Dutton Children's Books
New York

THE UNKNOWN WORLD

I magine that you are living in the distant past. You believe that the world is flat, and that if you travel too far you will fall off the edge—perhaps into a pit of fire. You also believe in giants, dragons, and six-headed serpents, and you think that there are people in distant lands who have two heads. Would you leave home to go exploring?

TO BOLDLY GO...

T he human race has an unquenchable curiosity about unknown places. Throughout history, people have risked everything to see what is on the other side of the hill, or the river, or the ocean. They do it for lots of reasons—for more land, for great riches, for adventure, for conquest and glory, or simply because it's there.

Have you got what it takes to be an explorer? Are you fit, healthy, determined, tough, single-minded, resourceful, a good leader, and possibly a little mad? Remember, you must not be a picky eater (you might have to try rats, polar bears, or locusts), and you can't be a scaredy-cat (you might meet a whirling Dervish or a dog-headed cannibal). If you are prone to homesickness, seasickness, or you are likely to miss your mother, your dog, or your teddy bear, don't try it—read about it instead.

THE LAND OF PUNT

One great voyage of discovery took place in the time of Queen Hatshepsut in Egypt almost 4,000 years ago. She was the only woman ever to be a Pharaoh, and she launched an expedition to the legendary Land of Punt. Her ships set sail down the Red Sea and round the horn of Africa to Somalia, where they landed. On their return, the sailors spread before the queen a huge array of rare and exotic goods. The Egyptian people were amazed by some of the treasures that were brought back, which included ebony, ivory, animal skins, incense, myrrh, white gold, monkeys, and baboons.

Egyptian sailors explored the seas and rivers of Africa

EMPIRE OF THE SEA

The Phoenicians lived in the land of Canaan about 3,000 years ago. Their land was small and barren, so they made their living from the sea. They became skilled navigators and traders, and were soon masters of the whole Mediterranean (a word that means "center of the world"). The Phoenicians were famous for making purple dye and beautiful glassware, which they traded everywhere in the known world. Their horse-headed ships were familiar in

A bearded–man pendant

every port in Europe. They explored the Black Sea and were probably the first seamen to sail all the way round the coast of Africa.

GOD OR MADMAN?

Alexander the Great is the most famous of the early explorers. He died at the comparatively young age of 32, having spent the previous 11 years rampaging his way from Greece to India, becoming ruler of the largest empire in the western world. Alexander was not a trader, he was a conqueror with a great desire to outdo all the great heroes of Greek myth. His huge army of 35,000 men (most of whom died in campaign) captured the whole of Persia before fighting its way through unexplored central Asia to the great river Indus. Alexander took with him scientists, engineers, map-makers, and

On this map, Marco Polo and his companions are seen riding across the desert on camels

"steppers"—men who measured distance by counting their steps. He founded 70 cities and insisted on being worshiped as a god!

MARCO MILLIONS

In 1271, at the age of 16, Marco Polo joined his father and uncle on a trip to the court of Kublai Khan, the great Mongol ruler who had conquered China. They traveled overland across Asia, through the Gobi desert, and over

When Marco Polo told the people in Europe what he had seen on his travels, they didn't believe him

the high Pamir mountains, following the bandit–infested Silk Route to the fabled land of Cathay (China). For the next 20 years, Marco Polo worked for Kublai Khan as a servant and spy. He claimed to have traveled throughout China and the South Seas. When he returned to Europe he wrote a book about his travels called *A Description of the World*.

"MARCO MILLIONS"

Back in his native Venice, Marco Polo was given the nickname "Marco Millions" because of his tendency to exaggerate wildly, but before he died he insisted, "I did not write half of what I saw."

What Marco said he saw:
1. Stones that burn like logs
2. Men with tails
3. Huge serpents
4. Cannibals with heads like dogs

What they might have been:
1. Lumps of coal
2. Monkeys
3. Giant lizards
4. ?

MAKING A COMPASS

Before you go exploring, you need to know which way you are facing. Make this simple compass using a needle that has been magnetized. The needle is magnetized when a paper clip sticks to it.

What you will need:
- Large needle
- Horseshoe magnet
- Knife (TAKE CARE)
- Bottle cork
- Water
- Shallow dish

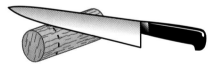

1. Hold the needle with the eye at the top. Stroke the needle downward a half dozen times with a magnet to magnetize it, making sure that north is at the top of the magnet.

2. Carefully slice a piece about 1/4 in (7 mm) from the end of the cork.

3. Taking great care not to prick your fingers, push the magnetized needle through the cork. Draw an arrow on the cork toward the point of your needle. This will be North. Make other marks around the cork to indicate South, East, and West.

4. Pour some water into a shallow dish and float your cork in it. You will find that the point of the needle swings round to north.

SEA ROVERS

Raiders, traders, pirates, and explorers, the Vikings were fearsome seafarers. They reached America 500 years before Columbus, and penetrated deep into Europe. The Vikings came from Norway, Sweden, and Denmark, where the land was rocky and the growing season short. They were always in search of new places to settle—or raid.

BERSERKERS

To go "a-viking" meant to become a pirate. There was a season for it—the Viking season—after spring planting and before the harvest. At this time, bands of men would go to sea on raiding expeditions. The speed and ferocity of their attacks made them greatly feared. They were possessed by a fighting madness during the raids that was known as going "berserk." Vikings were unafraid of death because they believed that a warrior who died in battle went straight to Valhalla, their name for Paradise.

ERIC THE RED

In AD 982, a violent red-headed Viking called Eric the Red was exiled from Norway for killing a man. He went to Iceland, but got into more trouble and was outlawed for another three years. He spent his time exploring an unknown ice-bound land to the west. This he called Greenland, a name he chose to encourage settlers to the icy region.

NEW FOUND LAND

Leif the Lucky was the eldest son of Eric the Red. Not so hot-headed as his father, he was nevertheless bold, clever, and a good sailor. Around the year AD 1,000, he set out to investigate sightings of a new land far beyond Greenland. He and his crew eventually made landfall on a great barren rock which was probably Baffin Island. They sailed on round the coast to a more promising site, which was possibly Labrador, that they called Markland (Forestland), and then, rounding a headland, they sailed up a river and made camp for the winter. It was here that one of Leif's crew discovered wild vines with grapes growing on them, a find that caused Leif to call

A STAR SIGN NORTH

On a clear, starry night, there was one sure way to find north. Try it yourself;
it works anywhere in the northern hemisphere.

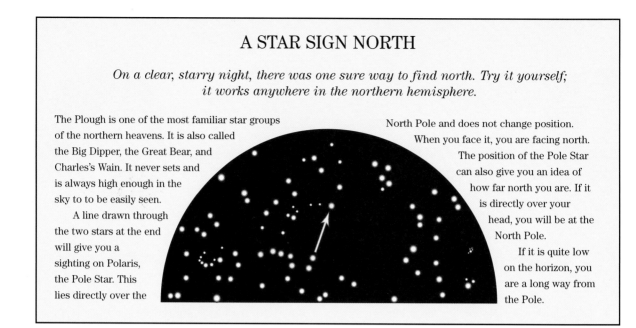

The Plough is one of the most familiar star groups of the northern heavens. It is also called the Big Dipper, the Great Bear, and Charles's Wain. It never sets and is always high enough in the sky to to be easily seen.

A line drawn through the two stars at the end will give you a sighting on Polaris, the Pole Star. This lies directly over the North Pole and does not change position. When you face it, you are facing north.

The position of the Pole Star can also give you an idea of how far north you are. If it is directly over your head, you will be at the North Pole.

If it is quite low on the horizon, you are a long way from the Pole.

---

the place Vinland. Today we know it as Newfoundland.

WAVE RIDERS

The longship with its long, lean outline gave the Vikings just the advantage they needed to raid wherever they pleased. It could sail in just over three feet of water (a meter), allowing the raiders to travel far up rivers. It was also sturdy enough to withstand the gales of the North Atlantic. The longship was about 75 feet long (23 meters) and powered by 16 pairs of oars and a large square sail. It usually had a high carved prow and was hung with shields. Proud of their ships, the Vikings gave them names like "Surf Dragon," "Oar-Steed," or "Wave Rider."

Shipboard life was hard. There were no cabins on a Viking longship, although a tent was sometimes put up amidships on a wooden

frame. The crew slept in a type of leather sleeping bag, sometimes two or three to a bag for warmth. For their meals they had dried meat and fish, soured butter, cheese, and beer.

WHERE IN THE WORLD...?

The Vikings were the first people to make long voyages across open sea out of sight of land, rather than hugging the coastlines as previous explorers had done. They had words for north, south, east, and west, but they had no compass and could only navigate by the sun and stars. They knew, for example, that the height of the sun at midday gave an indication of how far north they were, but when fog obscured both sun and stars, they were lost. Some sailors carried birds that they would set free to guide them toward land.

A Viking longship
out at sea

CIRCUMNAVIGATION

By the late fifteenth century, the news was out—the world was round, not flat! Not everyone believed it at first, but it was soon proved by some daring voyages. The fifteenth century was the great age of exploration when ambitious Europeans set sail across vast oceans in search of new lands, adventure, spices, and gold.

THE GREATEST JOURNEY

When the Portuguese captain Ferdinand Magellan set sail, his aim was to reach the fabulous Spice Islands (now known as the Moluccas) in the Pacific by a westward route. He did not intend a round-the-world trip, but that is how it turned out. The voyage was financed by the Spanish, who wanted to establish trade routes to the East and to claim new territory. Magellan left Spain in 1519 with 260 men and five ships. They carried lots of trading goods but, as it turned out, not nearly enough food.

SHIPWRECK AND MUTINY

Magellan's fleet crossed the Atlantic and sailed down the coast of South America looking for a westward route. They finally discovered a perilous sea passage to the Pacific, which we now call the Straits of Magellan. The weather was bitterly cold and rations were miserably short. This caused the crew to rebel and Magellan was forced to execute several men. Later, one of the ships was wrecked.

We know now that the Pacific Ocean covers one third of the earth's surface, but Magellan did not. It was wider by far than anyone could have imagined, and conditions for the fleet

A French sailor uses the stars to find his way

A master of a ship

grew worse and worse. For four months there was no fresh food on board. Twenty men starved to death and the rest were forced to eat maggoty ship's biscuits, boiled leather, sawdust, and rats, which were sold on board for half a ducat (a gold coin) each.

A TRAGIC END

Magellan himself never reached the Spice Islands. He was killed in the Philippines when he became involved in a quarrel between local chiefs. Sebastian del Cano took command of the 115 survivors and sailed on.

The two remaining ships loaded up with spices and set off for home, but only the *Victoria* arrived. Of the 260 men who set sail with Magellan, just 18 survived the first circumnavigation of the globe.

Five Out, One Back
Santiago: wrecked off South America
San Antonio: turned back during the Pacific crossing
Concepcion: scuttled in the Philippines
Trinidad: captured by the Portuguese on the journey home
Victoria: second smallest ship in the fleet, but the only one to sail round the world

TRAVELER'S TALES

An Italian survivor of Magellan's voyage, called Antonio Pigafetta, wrote a book about his experiences which was published two years after his return. He told of the terrible hardships that the ships' crews had endured—the storms and bitter cold, the rotten food and stinking water. He also described man-eating sharks and the strange electrical phenomenon of St Elmo's fire, which made the ship's mast look as if it was burning.

THE SPICE TRADE

One reason to risk life and limb getting to the Spice Islands was to capture the spice trade. All over Europe people were crazy for spices, and paid enormous prices for them. For centuries the Spice Islands were the main source of nutmegs, cinnamon, and cloves. After Magellan, Portuguese merchants built up a rich trade in these exotic substances.

Spices were very popular in the kitchen where all sorts of dishes, both sweet and savory, were crammed with nutmegs and cinnamon. Clove oil was also used as an antiseptic and as a treatment for toothache. Nutmegs and other spices were thought to be a useful fumigant against the plague.

Jewelers devised tiny pocket graters for nutmegs—boxes with hinged lids and grating surfaces, and a little compartment for the nut. No fashionable explorer would have been without a nutmeg to grate in his food, his mulled wine, or his porridge.

EL DRACO—THE DRAGON

Spain and Portugal had a virtual monopoly on Pacific trade in the mid-sixteenth century until England made a bid for a share. In the struggle for power over the following years, the name the Spanish dreaded most was that of Francis Drake, whom they called El Draco. Drake, like Magellan, was a talented and fearless sea captain. His most famous voyage was his circumnavigation of the world in 1577 to 1580 On his return, Queen Elizabeth I knighted him on board his ship, the *Golden Hind.* To the English he was a hero, but to the Spanish he was a hated pirate since he took every opportunity to attack their ships and raid their ports, making himself rich in the process.

SPICE ISLAND COOKIES

These cookies are made with the same spices that sailors journeyed across the world to find. To make the fish shapes, use a special cookie cutter or carefully trace the outline with a knife.

1. Sift the flour, spices, and baking soda into a large mixing bowl. Cut the butter into little chunks and rub it into the flour using your fingertips. When the mixture looks like breadcrumbs, stir in the sugar.

2. Pour the syrup into the mixture and add the beaten egg. Stir with a spoon until the mixture forms a dough.

4. Cut out some fish shapes then place them on a greased cookie sheet and bake in a pre-heated oven at 375°F/190°C for about 12 minutes, or until golden brown. When the cookies are cool, take them off the sheet and decorate them with icing patterns.

What you will need:
12 oz (350g) white flour
1/2 tsp baking soda
1 tsp ground cinnamon
1/2 tsp ground nutmeg
a pinch of ground cloves
4 oz (100g) butter
6 oz (175g) soft brown sugar
3 tbsp corn syrup
1 egg, beaten
tubes of colored icing

3. Knead the dough with your hands until it is smooth. Place it on a lightly floured board and roll it out to a thickness of about 1/4 in (5mm) thick.

THE NEW WORLD

Christopher Columbus had all the makings of a great explorer right from the start: he was obsessed, he was persistent, and he was ambitious. His big idea was that it was possible to get to the East by sailing west. Not many people believed him and he spent seven years trying to persuade the king and queen of Spain to lend him the money to try the idea out.

WOULD YOU TRUST THIS MAN WITH YOUR LIFE?

Ninety men agreed to sail off the edge of the map with Columbus, far into the distance where no European had been before. Why did they go? For fame and fortune.

Columbus was smart. His idea that the world was round and that it would be possible to get to Asia by a westward route, was quite correct. He was also an experienced sailor and had worked out that the trade winds would get him westwards faster if he set off from the Canary Islands rather than Spain. So far, so good. He crossed the Atlantic without any major mishaps and after 30 days made landfall in the Caribbean. He had discovered the edge of an unknown continent! The only problem was that he thought it was Japan.

WHERE IN THE WORLD?

Columbus set sail with a fleet of three ships, the *Pinta*, the *Niña* and the *Santa Maria*. None of them was longer than 82 feet (25 meters), which is tiny by modern standards, and the navigational equipment was very basic.

Columbus used an astrolabe to work out latitude (position north or south). It had a movable arm that could measure the height of the Pole Star above the horizon: the greater the angle, the further north the ship's position.

Position east or west was much more difficult and had to be calculated by "dead reckoning." This meant making estimates of three things: direction (indicated by compass), time (measured by sand glass), and speed which could not be measured, only guessed). At first Columbus overestimated the speed of the *Santa Maria* so his dead reckoning was not too

The Santa Maria

accurate, but later his skill improved. Also, he had the navigator's sixth sense, a precious gift, which usually got him where he wanted to go.

The *Santa Maria* carried a couple of ship's boys among the crew, children of 10 or 12 whose job it was to turn the sand glass that measured time. It took about 30 minutes for each glass to empty. A little chant went with the turning of the glass:

> *The watch is called,*
> *The glass floweth,*
> *We shall make good voyage*
> *If God willeth.*

THE ARAWAKS

Columbus was so convinced that he had reached Asia by a western route that he called the Caribbean "the Indies" and the inhabitants "Indians." They were in fact Arawaks who had

The king and queen of Spain welcome Columbus back from his voyage to the New World

lived quite happily in their "undiscovered" land before Columbus arrived to claim it for the king and queen of Spain. He was a little disappointed by their lack of wealth, since none of the Arawaks seemed to be dripping with gold jewelry as he had expected them to be. Nevertheless he returned to Spain with a number of interesting items including plants, parrots, and hammocks. Of these, the hammock proved to be very popular, especially with sailors who found it a very convenient and comfortable way to sleep on board ship.

A DISAPPOINTED MAN

Altogether Columbus made three journeys of exploration to the Caribbean, still believing it to be part of Asia. His great desire to find the fabulous wealth of China and Japan, as described by Marco Polo, was never realized and he died in poverty, a disappointed man. He did not even have the consolation of knowing that he had discovered an unknown continent.

CONQUISTADORS

Hernán Cortés was a Spanish adventurer. He and men like him were called *conquistadors*, the Spanish word for conquerors. Above all, they wanted gold. Cortés had heard stories of great riches to be found on the mainland of South America, so in 1519 he set sail for Mexico with 550 men and a few horses.

The ruling people in Mexico were the Aztecs, a powerful tribal group who built magnificent cities and had a rich culture of their own. Cortés was right about their wealth—the Aztecs made magnificent gold and silver jewelry as well as mosaics of turquoise, jade, and jet. Cortés was anxious to get his hands on this treasure, but the odds against him looked great. The Aztecs were powerful, well-armed and well-organized. To make sure that his men did not turn back, Cortés ordered all his ships to be sunk. It was all or nothing.

A mask of Quetzalcoatl

MAKING AN AZTEC MASK

Make your own Aztec mask out of papier-mâché—the name for a mixture of newspaper and paste. Instead of precious stones like turquoise, this mask is decorated with colored paper.

<table>
<tr><td>

What you will need:
- Balloon
- Vaseline
- Wallpaper paste
- Newspaper

</td><td>

- Scissors
- Thin cardboard
- Green poster paint
- Blue, green, black, and white paper
- String

</td></tr>
</table>

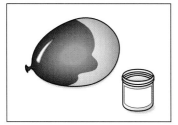

1. Blow up the balloon until it is as big as your face—you might need the help of an adult to inflate it completely. Rub the surface with a thin layer of Vaseline. (This will make it easier to remove the balloon in Step 3.)

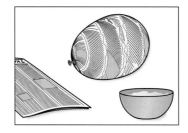

2. Mix 2 tbsp of wallpaper paste with water until it is the consistency of egg white. Tear the newspaper into strips about 2.5 cm (1 in) wide and 15 cm (6 in) long. Dip each strip into the paste before laying them across the balloon. Build up eight layers, then leave to dry for three or four days.

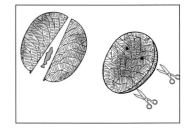

3. Cut the papier-mâché shape in half, put one half aside, and discard the balloon. Trim off any ragged edges top and bottom, and make eye holes.

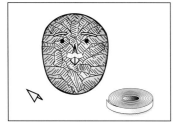

4. Cut a triangle from cardboard, fold it in half, and tape it to the middle of the mask to make a nose. Make eyebrows from strips of cardboard, and cover with a layer of papier-mâché. Leave to dry overnight.

5. Cut the blue and green paper into small squares and rectangles. Mix up some more wallpaper paste and add paint to make it dark green. Paint the paste onto the mask and stick on the paper shapes, avoiding the eye holes.

6. Finish the mask with a black paper mouth, and white paper teeth and eyes. (Make holes so that you can see.) Punch holes in each side of the mask, and thread string through them so that you can wear the mask.

THE PLUMED SERPENT

By a strange quirk of fate, Cortés and his men were made welcome by the Aztecs. This was partly because they were terrified of guns and horses, neither of which they had seen before, but also because they thought Cortés's arrival was that of the god Quetzalcoatl, known as the Plumed Serpent. According to Aztec myth, Quetzalcoatl was a ruler from the past who would one day come back to lead them. He had a white face, a black beard and wore a headdress of feathers. The pale-faced, black-bearded Cortés with his plumed helmet seemed to fit the bill.

GOLD AND FEATHERS

The Aztecs made exquisite gold and silver jewelry using simple tools of stone and copper. The Spanish were amazed by their skill, especially since they used no iron tools. Some of the most highly skilled craftsmen were the feather workers who created shields, fans, headdresses, and cloaks from the vividly colored feathers of tropical birds.

LOVE AND WAR

The Aztecs had many rivals among the neighboring tribes and Cortés tried to gain their support. He was helped when the daughter of one chieftain fell madly in love with him. She was known to the Spanish as Dona Marina or La Malinche. She learned Spanish and acted as Cortés's guide and interpreter, making his eventual conquest of the Aztecs much easier.

THE POWER OF LIFE AND DEATH

The Aztec emperor was Montezuma. He had an army of thousands of men and was fabulously wealthy. He observed religious customs which shocked the Spanish greatly. The Aztecs believed that the sun god died each night and would only be reborn the next day if he was fed with human blood. Consequently, they made daily human sacrifices. The sight of Aztec priests ripping the hearts out of living victims, and the temple steps running with blood, made Cortés believe he was justified in conquering their empire.

The Aztecs made daily sacrifices on the temple steps

THE FALL OF TENOCHTITLAN

Cortés besieged the great Aztec city of Tenochtitlán and it was only a matter of time before it fell. Food and water was cut off for nearly three months and countless thousands of the inhabitants died. Some of them starved to death, but many others died of European diseases such as measles and smallpox. Within a few years of the death of Montezuma, almost nothing was left of the great Aztec empire.

The Emperor Montezuma's body was thrown into the canal

THE SCIENTIFIC EXPLORER

The eighteenth century was the great age of science. Suddenly there was a huge curiosity about the world and a tremendous urge to have it measured, mapped, and named. Just how big was the Pacific Ocean? Were there people, places, animals, and plants that no European had ever seen before? It was to answer questions like these that Captain Cook set sail.

A SECRET MISSION

James Cook was given command of the most technological expedition of discovery to be mounted in the eighteenth century. A man of strong character and great intelligence, he was also an experienced sailor and, above all, a brilliant navigator. His first mission was to sail to the tiny island of Tahiti in the middle of the Pacific in order to observe a rare astronomical event—the planet Venus passing across the face of the sun. The reason for this was that such observations would give scientists a way of calculating the distance of the earth from the sun. But Cook carried with him a sealed envelope to be opened after his

astronomical observations were complete. It contained secret orders for another mission: to explore the South Pacific for a fifth continent, the mysterious "Terra Australis" and to claim it for Britain.

Captain James Cook

THE ENDEAVOUR

Cook's ship, the *Endeavour*, was a converted coal ship, a tubby little vessel but strongly built and provided with all the latest scientific equipment. She carried a crew of 94 including an astronomer, a naturalist, a botanist, and two artists. Cook carried the most up-to-date compass, a reflection telescope, and a surveying instrument called a theodolite to help him with his navigational and astronomical calculations.

LIMEYS

As part of the scientific approach to the expedition, Cook took some trouble over provisioning the ship. He knew that sailors on long sea voyages often suffered from a nasty disease called scurvy. This was caused by a severe lack of vitamin C, although no one knew that at the time. Cook's method of combating the disease was to give the crew pickled cabbage and syrup of oranges and lemons. On his second voyage he tried a delicious concoction called carrot marmalade.

As well as food supplies, there was another cargo: trading items for making friends in the South Pacific. Among these were scissors, iron nails, mirrors, axe heads, glass beads, fishing hooks, and dolls.

live sheep
salt pork
ship's biscuit
oranges
suet
vinegar
wine
salt beef
live pigs
onions
salt
sugar
oil
mustard seed
live chickens
dried fruit
flour
lemons
rum
dried peas
beer

Eventually, by a process of trial and error the British Navy decided that the best protection against scurvy was fresh lime juice, a treatment that earned British sailors the nickname "limeys."

NEW TECHNOLOGY

In 1714 the British Navy announced a competition with a large cash prize for the first person to make a clock suitable for keeping time at sea. The only clocks then available were pendulum clocks which were fine on dry land but useless on the rolling deep. The competition was won by John Harrison with his spring-driven chronometer, a brilliant device that kept extremely good time and allowed navigators to calculate longitude (position east/west) with great accuracy.

John Harrison's chronometer

TERRA AUSTRALIS

Captain Cook first sailed to New Zealand where he got a very hostile reception from the local people, the Maoris. Their warriors had elaborate facial tattoos designed to impress their enemies, and at one point the *Endeavour* was chased by hundreds of war canoes. Luckily Cook was able to establish friendly relations with other Maoris further north. He was unusual among European explorers at the time

in having great respect for the people he met, although he was slightly alarmed by the Maori habit of eating their captured enemies.

After completing his circumnavigation of New Zealand, Cook sailed for the unknown coast of Australia which he followed for hundreds of miles. He landed at an inlet on the east coast which he named Botany Bay because of the many botanical specimens he found there. This became the landing place for many ships after him. Terra Australis was on the map.

LIFE ABOARD

Life aboard ship was very disciplined—it had to be when so many people were living and working in a small space. Each person had his own job whether it was swabbing the decks or cooking the meals. Ship life was divided into "watches" signalled by ringing a bell. A watch was a period of four hours. While one watch was on duty the other was off. The dawn watch had to scrub the decks, the next watch pumped water out the bilges (the lowest part of the ship). Throughout the day, sailors ran up the rigging, trimmed the sails, spliced the ropes, and generally made sure that everything was kept shipshape.

parrots that they would teach to speak. Others just got drunk. On Cook's ship the boatswain's assistant died after drinking a quart of neat rum.

A drawing of a monkey by Alexander von Humboldt

"WHAT SHALL WE DO WITH THE DRUNKEN SAILOR?"

For recreation sailors often took up scrimshaw, carving intricate patterns into shells or walrus tusks. Others took up fancy knotwork and made their own hammocks. Often there was a fiddler aboard who provided musical accompaniment for singsongs or dancing the hornpipe. Sometimes sailors collected exotic goods like beautiful shells, or Polynesian

HUMBOLDT

One of the greatest scientific explorers of the eighteenth century was Alexander von Humboldt, a German who explored the interior of South America. He was an immensely talented man—a linguist, an astronomer, a geologist, and a botanist. He had the sort of unquenchable curiosity that kept him going through impossible terrain. He explored steamy jungles, scorching deserts and mile-high mountains. In 1802 he reached Quito, one of the highest cities in the world. Further south in Peru, he studied the remains of Inca civilization that had been wiped out by the conquistadors. Wherever he went he kept detailed accounts of the animals, birds, and plants he saw. One of the things he recorded was the steady current of cold water that flows along the Peruvian coast carrying rich stocks of fish. It was named the Humboldt Current in his honor.

MAKING A SEA CHEST

Sailors took their possessions to sea in a chest that was stored below decks. It had to be strong to withstand buffeting at sea, and it had to have handles so that it was easy to carry. Here's how to make a chest of your own to keep your most precious possessions safe.

What you will need:
- Strong cardboard box with a lid
- Scissors
- Thin and thick cardboard
- Dinner plate
- Tape
- Glue
- Prong paper fasteners
- Paint
- String

1. Cut one long edge off the box lid and throw it away. Make hinges from thick cardboard and fasten the lid to the box with prong paper fasteners.

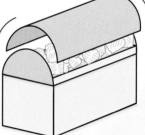

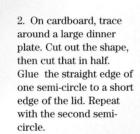

2. On cardboard, trace around a large dinner plate. Cut out the shape, then cut that in half. Glue the straight edge of one semi-circle to a short edge of the lid. Repeat with the second semi-circle.

3. With the lid down, fill the area between the two semi-circles with scrunched up newspaper. Next, curve a piece of thin cardboard over the lid and tape it to the edges.

4. Paint the box to look like wood. To make a lock for your chest, cut out an oblong and an arrow from thick cardboard. Paint them and attach them to the box and the lid with prong paper fasteners as shown.

5. Thread some string through holes in the short sides of the box, and knot it on the inside to make handles. Decorate the chest with more prong paper fasteners.

RIVER EXPLORATION

Great rivers were always an attraction to early explorers because they provided a natural highway into the heart of the continent. It was possible to make good speed on water, and it was much easier to carry the necessary gear. There were hidden dangers, however, like crocodiles, hippopotami, rapids, and arguments with the crew.

THE RIVER OF LIFE

The great River Nile had been known since ancient times where it flowed through Egypt and out into the Mediterranean. But the origins of the river remained one of the great geographical mysteries until well into the nineteenth century. There were lots of theories about it, and several explorers had tried to follow it upstream from Egypt, but all had been defeated by distance, heat, fearful swamps, and—most deadly of all—malarial fever.

In 1856, the Royal Geographical Society in London appointed two young men to approach the problem from the other end. Richard Burton and John Hanning Speke set out for the east coast of Africa in order to find the source of the Nile among the great lakes of Uganda.

CHALK AND CHEESE

Burton and Speke were very different characters, and in time these differences began to tell. Burton was an intellectual, spoke many languages, and had written several books. He had been a soldier in India, and was the first European to visit the Muslim holy city of Mecca. Speke, on the other hand, was unknown, untraveled, quiet, and rather shy. The thing that the two men had in common was ambition.

Burton and Speke mounted their expedition and set off into the unknown. Despite exhaustion and extreme illness, they finally reached their destination, Lake Ujiji (Lake Tanganyika) which they believed to be the source of the Nile. To their disappointment, they discovered that the only river connected

to the lake flowed in, not out. It was clearly not the Nile. Speke set off alone for another lake to the north that no other European had ever seen.

Richard Burton wore Arab clothes when he went to Mecca

LAKE VICTORIA

The lake was as big as an ocean and, in true explorer style, Speke named it after the queen. He was overjoyed when he realized that the big river flowing out of it was probably the source of the Nile. He raced back to tell Burton the news but, as he might have expected, his friend was jealous and absolutely furious!

THE RIVALS

A huge row broke out between the men, especially when Speke returned to England and spread the news of their discovery, claiming all the glory for himself. He was appointed to lead another expedition to Lake Victoria and, although Speke investigated the river flowing northward from the lake, Burton disputed that it actually was the Nile. A public discussion was arranged where the two men would meet face to face and thrash the matter out. But on the day before the meeting, Speke was found dead from a mysterious shooting accident. There were rumors of suicide—some thought that Speke had felt unable to face the intellectual brilliance of Burton. But, in the end, other explorers proved him right. Lake Victoria really *was* where the Nile began.

A SURVIVAL KIT

When John Speke explored the Nile, he had the help of an army of bearers to carry his gear. Here are just some of the things he took with him:

- An enamel bath
- Rifles and pistols for hunting and protection
- Beads, silk cloth, blankets, and watches for gifts or trading
- A Persian rug
- Canned food from Fortnum & Mason (a fancy London store)
- An iron chair
- A boat made in five sections that could be assembled for going upriver
- Canvas tents and other camping equipment
- Medicine chests

You will have to carry your own gear when you go exploring, so travel light. Fill a medium-sized container, say a lunch box, with essential items. Here are a few ideas:

- A compass—to find out where you are
- A flashlight and some spare batteries—for exploring in dark places
- Matches—to light a fire
- A candle—so that you don't waste too many matches when you light the fire
- Some Band-Aids—in case you get blisters
- String—in case your shoelaces break
- A penknife—to cut the string
- A fish hook and line—to catch your dinner
- A huge slab of chocolate—in case you don't catch any fish

THE HEART OF AFRICA

The vast interior of Africa was unknown to Europeans until the mid-nineteenth century. Travel was impeded by thick jungles, wild animals, and poisonous insects. The danger of it attracted many would-be explorers, but there was one in particular who captured the public imagination, becoming a legend in his own lifetime.

The Ma Robert

DAVID LIVINGSTONE

Born in an overcrowded slum in Glasgow, Scotland, David Livingstone spent his childhood working 13 hours a day in a cotton mill. Yet he still found time to educate himself and qualify as a doctor. In 1841 he achieved his ambition of being sent to Africa as a medical missionary, returning home only twice in the next 30 years. Explorer, geographer, astronomer, botanist, and chemist, Livingstone traveled all over the African continent on foot. He was inspired by the idea of eradicating slavery, still a brutal trade in many parts of Africa. He believed that opening up the continent to foreign influence would cause the slave trade to collapse.

SHEER GRIT

Livingstone's first attempt at exploration nearly ended in disaster when he took his wife and children across the Kalahari desert. They all nearly died when the expedition ran out of food and water. After that, he sent them back to England and continued his explorations alone. He was not put off the task even when savaged by a lion whose teeth left a row of holes like bullet wounds in his arm. Despite recurring illness and serious attacks of malaria, Livingstone continued his travels until he died.

UP THE ZAMBEZI

Following the great Zambezi river, Livingstone became the first European to cross Africa from coast to coast. Many of the people he met had not seen a white face before and were amazed by his clothing and equipment. His hairbrush, his matches, and his lantern were objects of great curiosity and caused him to be treated as a magician.

In trying to convert the Africans to Christianity, he sometimes presented a magic lantern show of scenes from the bible, but more often than not it was feared as something supernatural and his audience ran away.

In the territory of the Balonda tribe, Livingstone found that many of the local chiefs were women. One of them wanted to divert him from his route in order to pay a visit to her brother Shiute, the great Balonda chief. Livingstone politely declined, but the Balonda woman insisted. In fact, she

Stanley and his bearers go in search of Livingstone

led the way herself. Livingstone, a prim Victorian unused to women taking command, was outraged, most particularly by her "frightful nudity" since she was covered only in body paint and jewelry.

THE SMOKE THAT THUNDERS

In 1856 Livingstone discovered the stupendous falls on the Zambezi which were known to the local people as "the smoke that thunders." In the manner of European explorers, he renamed them the Victoria Falls after the queen of Britain. The news of this soon reached home and when he finally returned to England on a visit, he found that he was a national hero and was introduced to the queen herself.

A further expedition up the Zambezi with a converted paddle steamer called the *Ma Robert* ended in failure when the boat could not get past the rapids. But Livingstone would not be discouraged and made another

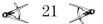

attempt soon after. No one heard word of him for the next three years, and many people thought he was dead. Public interest was so great that a young journalist on the *New York Herald* was dispatched to Africa with a mission—FIND LIVINGSTONE!

HENRY MORTON STANLEY

The journalist in question was Henry Morton Stanley. He was a bit of a mystery man, having run away from home at the age of 16 and changed his name. After a few shady adventures such as fighting for both sides in the American Civil War, he became a journalist. Bold, aggressive, and decisive, he was just the man for a mission in central Africa.

It was two years before Stanley achieved his objective of locating the elusive David Livingstone. After an arduous journey fraught with difficulties he finally met up with him on the shores of Lake Tanganyika. Wearing a freshly pressed linen suit, polished boots, and a gleaming white hat, Stanley approached the famous man with four words of greeting: "Doctor Livingstone, I presume?"

This phrase haunted Stanley for the rest of his life. It became a bit of a joke, and cartoons of it appeared in the newspapers. People meeting him for the first time would always say, "Mr. Stanley, I presume?"

UP THE ZAIRE

David Livingstone died in Africa not long after this famous meeting and Stanley returned home and wrote a book about his adventures that became an immediate bestseller. But the exploring bug had got him and he soon returned to Africa to take an expedition up the great Zaire river. Starting in Zanzibar, he recruited over two hundred people as porters for the trip (one of them turned out to be a mass-murderer, but Stanley only found that out later). Many of them had to carry a portable boat that came in sections and which was named the *Lady Alice* after Stanley's sweetheart.

JUNGLE!

The dense jungle of equatorial Africa was a bit of a shock. Tropical vegetation closed in on Stanley's expedition like a black wall, shutting out the sun. Dew dripped from every leaf, clothes got soaked, helmets felt like lead; there was heat and fever and the fear of cannibals.

As if this was not enough, the Zaire river suddenly plunged over a series of cataracts studded with deadly black rocks like teeth. These rapids claimed the lives of many of Stanley's expedition including a young African boy called Kalulu whom Stanley had adopted.

"Doctor Livingstone, I presume?"

ARE YOU THE EXPLORING TYPE?

To be an explorer you need to be fit, tough, decisive, foolhardy, obsessive, brave, and a little mad.
Answer the following questions to find out whether you have what it takes.

- You've got malaria and blisters and there are still 20 miles to base camp. Do you:
  A break into a jog
  B lie down till you feel better
  C cry

- Some of your party are grumbling about the conditions. Do you:
  A crack the whip
  B execute the ring leaders
  C say sorry

- You find a scorpion in your shoe. Do you:
  A swat it with a rolled up newspaper
  B make a quick anatomical drawing of it
  C faint

- A tribe of dog-headed cannibals come to your camp and demand gifts. Do you:
  A fire a rifle over their heads
  B offer them some beads
  C run away

- Some of your party are losing heart. Do you:
  A say you hate them and why don't they go home
  B give them extra rations
  C sulk

- The rope bridge over a raging torrent looks a bit frayed. Do you:
  A go over first to test its strength
  B send the fattest person over at gunpoint
  C panic

- You've run out of food and water. Do you:
  A shoot your pet dog and eat it
  B boil up a nice dish of locusts
  C starve

EXPLORER'S HEADGEAR

The best-dressed explorer never went out without a hat. The favorite hat for Victorian explorers in hot countries was the solah topee, also known as the pith helmet. This was invented in India and named after the Hindi word for hat which is *topee.* It was made from the pith of the solah plant which had excellent insulating properties and would stop you getting sunstroke in the most blistering heat. Like a motorbike helmet, the topee had webbing inside to fit round your head. It was covered in white cotton cloth to deflect the sun's rays. It had only one disadvantage—it was incredibly uncomfortable to wear!

ANSWERS
Mainly As: You are fearless and a little crazy and would make an excellent explorer.
Mainly Bs: You are practical, take a sensible approach to most problems, and would make a good tour guide.
Mainly Cs: You are too faint-hearted to be an adventurer. Stay home and read about exploring instead.

GREAT CROSSINGS

By 1800, the outlines of the world's continents were known. Most of them had been circumnavigated and plotted on the map. It was time to fill in the blank bits in the middle. Crossing the interior of the great land masses of Australia and America took a particular type of explorer—fit, tough, brave, and adventurous—and even these qualities were not always enough...

Meriwether Lewis

A DARLING PROJECT

When Thomas Jefferson was President of the United States in 1801 there were only 16 states in the Union and these were all in the eastern part of the country. Jefferson was determined to find out what the rest of the country was like so he made plans for an expedition to find a route to the west coast. He appointed a young man called Meriwether Lewis as the expedition leader. Lewis had been in the army and was just the sort of man to enjoy an adventure. He called it "a darling project." His co-commander was an army friend called William Clark and together they chose a party of about 30 soldiers to accompany them.

WESTWARD HO!

Setting out from St Louis, which was then a small frontier town of a few hundred people, Lewis and Clark planned to follow the Missouri river to its source and from there to make an overland connection with the Columbia river which they knew flowed into the Pacific. They guessed that there might be mountains in between, but they had no idea how big those mountains would be!

Lewis and Clark had some nasty encounters with bears

BIRD WOMAN

The expedition paddled its way up the Missouri to the villages of the Mandan Indians where they wintered. On the way they had a few encounters with the Sioux who were not always friendly, but luckily no fighting broke out. In Mandan territory they were joined by a new expedition member who turned out to be one of the most valuable: a Shoshoni girl called Sacajawea, or Bird Woman. She accompanied Lewis and Clark across thousands of miles acting as guide and interpreter.

OVER THE ROCKIES

Crossing the Rockies with no sign of a trail was the hardest part of the trip. The snow-covered peaks seemed to go on forever. The going was tough, the nights bitterly cold, and food was in short supply. They had to cut their way through thick undergrowth and their feet were cut to pieces by the spikes of prickly pears. They passed through the lands of the Clatsops, the Nez Perce, and the Chinook. With few exceptions, the local tribes offered help and friendship. Lewis and Clark did not know it, but by forging a route to the west coast they were signing the death warrant of the Native American cultures they had the privilege to see.

Eventually the expedition reached the great Columbia river and paddled toward the coast. As winter was closing in, they smelled the sea air and heard the sound of the surf: the Pacific Ocean was ahead of them. They were the first white men to travel from coast to coast.

ACROSS THE OUTBACK

In 1859 the Australian government offered a prize to the first person to cross the continent from south to north, and the challenge was taken up by Robert Burke and William Wills. Burke was a gold prospector, an adventurous man with a hot temper. He had no experience of life in the outback and to many he seemed an odd choice as expedition leader.

The explorers equipped themselves with 24 camels imported from India, 23 horses, 12 tents, several carts, 80 pairs of boots and several gallons of rum, which was believed to keep the camels in good condition!

COOPER'S CREEK

On their journey Burke and Wills saw huge lizards, scorpions, snakes, bulldog ants, and armies of rats. When they made camp at Cooper's Creek in the center of the continent, they were almost eaten alive by mosquitoes. The expedition passed through desert and scrub, through plains and woods, and over rocky ridges. They got within sight and smell of the north coast, but found their way blocked by mangrove swamps. They had to turn back without seeing the sea.

The return journey was a nightmare of bad weather and dwindling supplies. One by one the camels had to be shot and eaten. Only three members of the expedition made it alive to Cooper's Creek where they thought supplies were waiting. To their horror, they found a note to say that the supply train had moved out eight hours earlier, thinking they were dead. Burke and Wills died in the bush, leaving only one survivor of the first attempt to cross Australia from coast to coast.

NATIVE AMERICAN PICTURE WRITING

When Lewis and Clark traveled across America, they recorded their experiences with words. The local people they met used a different way of recording important events—pictures. They painted these pictures on animal hides, bark, and stone, using them to decorate shields, drums, and tepees. Here are some symbols for you to copy.

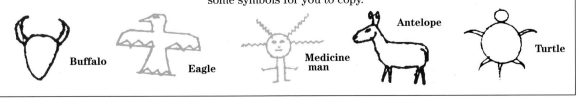

Buffalo

Eagle

Medicine man

Antelope

Turtle

Extracts from the Diary of Piers Gurney, Explorer, Somewhere in Africa

April 17th, 1861

We are covered from head to foot in red dust. There are vultures overhead and the plains simply teem with wildlife. Everywhere we see enormous herds of antelope and zebra, and quite often giraffes browsing among the trees. Our party continues in good heart, the bearers constantly singing and only occasionally quarreling.

May 25th

We have reached the hills and the air is fresher. The bearers complain of toiling uphill with their burdens, but the country is lush and bright with sub-tropical blossom. My botanist companion, Charles Lawrence, spends the evenings drawing the best specimens. The local tribespeople are suspicious of us, but inclined to be friendly when we offer to trade with iron nails and scissors.

June 19th

At last! We have reached the great Mbongo river. We have had to hack our way through dense undergrowth and there is much complaining in the ranks. I have had to settle many disputes – an unpleasant task which I carry out with much gesticulating and shouting. Charles tells me I missed a great career on the stage! We are now engaged in putting together the boat that we carried here in sections. From now on our progress should be faster. This evening I celebrated with a long soak in my tin bath.

July 12th

We make good progress but the weather continues unbearably hot and my pith helmet is devilishly uncomfortable. There is such moisture in the atmosphere that the jungle steams in the morning sun. Every kind of biting insect has attacked us. I tried to cheer up the party with an evening of magic-lantern pictures projected on to a makeshift screen fashioned from a sheet. Alas, it was not the success I had hoped for. Most of the bearers regarded the pictures of London and New York as magic of a particularly potent kind, and disappeared into the darkness, shrieking.

August 1st

The river has plunged toward the sea in a series of stupendous cataracts. The spray from the falls is visible for many miles so we had time to tie up the boat before we plunged over the edge. We attempted to take canoes down some of the quieter stretches between the cataracts but the current was too strong and we lost three men.

August 21st

The river has worn out its temper and now runs smooth as silk towards the open sea. We can almost smell the salt air. Looking in my shaving mirror today I see I am not a pretty sight! Gaunt with fever and sunburnt to a deep mahogany brown, I doubt whether my dear mother would recognize me.

September 8th

I have seen the waves breaking on the western coast of Africa! However, there was some sadness in our celebrations around the campfire. Many of us thought of the companions that we lost on the way. Trusty Charles Lawrence is still with us, praise be, and tonight he shared out the last box of Abernathy biscuits.

THE ENDS OF THE EARTH

*B*y the end of the nineteenth century, explorers were running out of places to go. Almost every corner of the world had been discovered and mapped. But there were two places that remained mysterious—the frozen wastes at the world's ends, the North and South Poles. The explorers who led the way were Nansen, Amundsen, and Scott.

THE UNBREAKABLE SHIP

No one knew if the North Pole was land or sea. They only knew for certain that it was icy. One explorer who tried to find out was a Norwegian, Fridtjof Nansen. He designed a ship that could withstand the pressures of the ice, rising up when it was frozen rather than cracking like a nut. He called it the *Fram* (Forward) and planned to sail it in

Nansen arrives at the North Pole with his dogs and sleds

the Arctic Ocean, allowing it to drift with the ice. By September 1893 the *Fram* was indeed locked solid and had to go with the ice flows. The process was painfully slow, and Nansen set off for the Pole with dog sleds across the ice. He had to give up within 240 miles of his objective because the ice started to break up. By pure chance he came across an English exploring team who took him back to Norway in their ships. The *Fram* arrived safely a few weeks later with the rest of the crew.

It was an African American, Matthew Henson, who reached the North Pole first. He raised the stars and stripes, and even dug a hole in the ice to prove that the North Pole was covered by sea.

THE ICY SOUTH

Conditions facing explorers to the South Pole were even more hazardous than those at the North. This was land—a whole continent with mountain ranges, glaciers, and valleys covered in packed ice. Most treacherous of all were the hidden crevasses that could suddenly pitch a man hundreds of feet down sheer cliffs of ice. And because it was so dangerous, there was no shortage of explorers wishing to go.

THE RIVALS

In the year 1911, two men led separate expeditions to reach the South Pole. One was a Norwegian who set sail in Nansen's old ship, the *Fram*. He was Roald Amundsen, a man who had set himself the task of mastering all the skills an Antarctic explorer would need. It was rumored that he even slept with the windows open during the subzero Norwegian winters to inure himself to the cold. His rival

Roald Amundsen in traditional Inuit clothing

was an Englishman, Robert Scott, a captain in the Royal Navy who had led previous expeditions to Antarctica, and had been closer to the South Pole than anyone else before. Both men were determined to be the first to the Pole.

THE RACE

The two teams set up base camps on the edge of Antarctica and spent the first months establishing supply lines for the final assault. They both knew that blizzards or injuries could wreck their chances and even kill them outright. It was a desperate gamble—and they were prepared to bet with their lives. Scott had the advantage of following a route that had been partly pioneered before. He also had three kinds of transport—tractor sleds, ponies, and dogs. Amundsen, on the other hand, was 60

Amundsen's men raise the Norwegian flag

miles closer to the Pole at his base camp, and was better prepared for the intense cold. His team wore light waterproof clothes of seal skin and furs like the Inuit, and they relied entirely on dogs for their transport.

RAISING THE FLAG

Scott's tractor sleds soon broke down, and the ponies could not withstand the bitter cold. He

was forced to use dog sleds for a while, but he did not have Amundsen's skill in handling them. Eventually he split his team in two and, with only four companions, pressed on for the Pole on foot. When he reached it on January 18th 1912, he found to his bitter disappointment that the Norwegian flag was already flying. Amundsen had arrived at the South Pole a month earlier, on December 14th 1911.

TRAGEDY

Amundsen and his team returned to base camp safely by the end of January, but Scott's return journey was overtaken by a series of disasters. Blizzards struck with blinding force, food supplies ran low, and the men staggered on with frostbitten feet. One team member died after a fall, and another after crippling frostbite. The rest were left weathering out a blizzard for nine days until they too died, of weakness, hypothermia, and starvation. They were within a few miles of their supply camp. Their bodies were found by a search party later that year.

Amundsen went on to sail right round the Arctic Ocean, but tragically he too was claimed by the ice two years later when the airship he was traveling in disappeared on a trip over the Arctic.

Captain Scott (center) with his team in the Antarctic

WHERE NEXT?

*I*n the past, people believed that monsters, dragons, and magical things lay beyond the horizon. In the same way, they saw the sun, moon, and stars as objects of mystery and power. To us, the sky represents the last horizon. And since the keen explorer can't be stopped, the only way is up—into the solar system, the galaxy, and the deep reaches of space.

Edwin Aldrin on the moon

COMPETITION IS THE SPUR

*L*ike the race for the Poles, the race for space has been hotly contested. The first liquid-fueled rocket was launched into space in 1926 by an American scientist named Robert Goddard. But within the next 35 years, Russian scientists caught up and launched the first man into space. Yuri Gagarin orbited the earth in 1961 in his spaceship Vostok 1. He was followed by the first woman into space, Valentina Tereshkova in 1963.

ONE SMALL STEP

A breath-taking event in 1969 captured the imagination of the whole world—for two hours there really was a man in the moon! The spacecraft Apollo 11 landed in the center of the visible side of the moon, in a place known as the Sea of Tranquility, and a crew member stepped out on to the barren rock. Neil Armstrong placed his feet where no human being had trodden before. And like all great explorers before him, he planted a flag.

Since then, unmanned craft have landed on Mars and Venus, and others have penetrated the cold outer reaches of our solar system to send back arrestingly beautiful pictures of Jupiter and Saturn.

EVEN FURTHER

Modern radio-telescopes can now penetrate unbelievable distances into space, receiving radio waves from galaxies millions of light years from our own. They have also discovered some of the dragons and monsters of outer space—red dwarfs, pulsars, and black holes. In the history of exploration, a new chapter has just begun...

The earth rises above the moon's horizon